D0560513

Disney's Year Book 1985

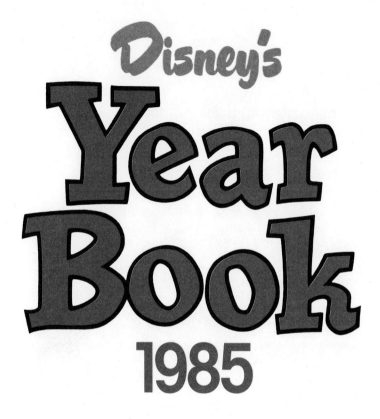

Disney's Year Book 1985

GROLIER ENTERPRISES INC.
Danbury, Connecticut

GROLIER ENTERPRISES INC.
Robert B. Clarke   *Publisher*

ISBN: 0-7172-8147-7
ISSN: 0273-1274

Stories on pages 12–23, 32–43, 56–67, 84–95, and all
Disney character illustrations
Copyright © 1985 by Walt Disney Productions

Copyright © 1985 by Grolier Inc.
Copyright © 1985 in Canada by Grolier Limited

No part of this book may be reproduced without special
permission in writing from the publishers

PRINTED IN THE UNITED STATES OF AMERICA

Illustration Credits and Acknowledgments

6–10—© Walt Disney Productions; 24—NASA; 25—Courtesy of Martin
Marietta; 26—Special thanks to the Smithsonian Institute; 27—NASA;
28—1984 Neil Leifer/Camera 5; 29—Bart Bartholomew/© 1984 Black Star;
31—Ken Regan/Camera 5; 44—© Duomo/Adam J. Stottman 1984; 46—John
Ficara/Newsweek; 47—© Duomo/Paul J. Sutton 1984; 48—© Duomo/David
Madison 1984; 49—© Charles G. Summers Jr./DPI; 50—Jean-Paul Ferrero/
Ardea London Ltd.; 51—left, Margot Conte/Animals Animals, right, S.J.
Krasemann/Peter Arnold; 52–53—Courtesy of Ford Motor Company;
54—left, Michael Melford/Wheeler Pictures, right, Courtesy of General
Motors; 55—Michael Melford/Wheeler Pictures; 68–71—Courtesy of
Scholastic Photography Awards, conducted by Scholastic Magazines, Inc.
and sponsored by Eastman Kodak Company; 72–74—Jenny Tesar;
75–79—Artist, Susan M. Waitt; 80—left, P. Morris/Ardea London Ltd., right,
© Owen Newman/Nature Photographers Ltd.; 81—Joe McDonald/Bruce
Coleman; 82—Jeff Foott/Bruce Coleman; 83—left, Joe McDonald/Animals
Animals, right, Michael and Barbara Reed/Animals Animals

Contents

Without a doubt, he is history's most famous duck. He's starred in the comics, on TV, and in more than 150 films—and he's won an Academy Award. In 1984, he celebrated his 50th birthday, and kids and grown-ups all over the world wished Donald Duck "many happy returns."

Why is Donald so popular? As anyone who knows and loves him has to admit, he's a feathered fumbler with lots of faults. He loses his temper, gets red as a beet, and

hops up and down with anger. He's a
loudmouth. (But we all love the special way
he talks.) And he frequently makes
mistakes—big mistakes. So what if Donald
isn't perfect? He's funny, friendly, frisky,
and fabulous.

Donald Duck was created by Walt Disney

*In a relaxed moment, Donald celebrates his 50th
birthday by posing with his creator, Walt Disney.*

in the early 1930s, and he quickly waddled his way to stardom. Daisy Duck soon came along, to be followed by Donald's three mischievous nephews—Huey, Dewey, and Louie. Later, other characters like Gyro Gearloose, a wacky inventor, and Scrooge

A scene from "The Wise Little Hen," Donald's first cartoon, which was released in 1934.

At Disney theme parks, Donald makes new friends.

McDuck, a jillionaire uncle, joined the Donald Duck family.

Soon Donald and his supporting cast were appearing in full-length feature films, such as *The Reluctant Dragon* (1941) and *The Three Caballeros* (1945), which combined live action and animation.

Donald found romance when Daisy Duck came along. She was featured in many of his later films.

As Donald's popularity soared he was given his own comic strip. Donald Duck merchandise, from dolls to orange juice to lamps, was snapped up by his fans. Donald made his television debut in 1954 and went on to appear daily on "The Mickey Mouse Club."

At 50, Donald Duck shows no signs of

slowing down. He is still delighting TV viewers as the host of "Donald Duck Presents" on the Disney cable channel. He continues to greet visitors personally at Disneyland in California, at Walt Disney World in Florida, and at Tokyo Disneyland in Japan. And he's still making movies.

Busy as he was, Donald still had plenty of time to celebrate his birthday. And what a celebration it was! A special plane, Duck One, carried Donald and Daisy on a four-day coast-to-coast tour. At Disneyland and at Walt Disney World, Donald starred in special musical variety shows and led parades of costumed characters down Main Street through showers of ticker tape. There were numerous other special celebrations as well.

Starting his second 50 years, Donald remains unchanged by success. He's still the same bumbling, hot-tempered but charming guy he always was, ready to explode in entertainingly comic rage when things go wrong. And they always do!

PINOCCHIO'S NOSE KNOWS

Pinocchio burst into Geppetto's shop. "Father!" he called out. "Where are you?"

"In my workshop," answered Geppetto.

Pinocchio dropped his schoolbooks and skipped back to his father's workroom. Geppetto was painting something. Pinocchio had to stand on his tiptoes to see what it was.

"What a pretty little girl!" he said.

"It's a puppet, Pinocchio," his father said.

Geppetto danced the marionette across the floor. He thought she was the prettiest puppet he had ever made.

"May I play with her, Father?" asked Pinocchio.

"No," replied Geppetto. "I made her for Mr. Santos, the puppeteer."

Pinocchio was disappointed.

Geppetto put on his coat. "I have to go out for an hour, Pinocchio," he said. "Now don't touch the puppet."

"Yes, Father," answered Pinocchio.

"Well, Pinoke," said Jiminy Cricket. "Time to do your homework."

"Okay," said Pinocchio. He began to practice his alphabet. But soon he got up.

"What's the matter?" asked Jiminy.

"Oh, nothing," Pinocchio answered. "I just feel like walking around a little." He wandered over to watch Cleo swim in circles. He sat down to watch Figaro's whiskers twitch.

Then Pinocchio wandered into Geppetto's workroom. He ran his fingers along the edge of the workbench. He kicked at some wood shavings under the bench.

"Come on, Pinoke," called Jiminy. "Finish your homework."

"I'll be right there," said Pinocchio.

Then Pinocchio pulled the red-headed puppet off the bench. "Father won't mind," he told himself. But she crashed to the floor in a tangle of strings.

"What's that?" called Jiminy.

"Oh, nothing," said Pinocchio. "I just dropped something."

Pinocchio picked up the new puppet. One of her arms had come off.

Gripping her close to his chest, Pinocchio saw the end of a string sticking out from her shoulder. He pulled on it until he had enough, and tied the arm back on.

"The other arm kind of sticks out," he said to himself, "but Father will never notice." Then he looked at the puppet's face. He gasped. The paint hadn't been dry, and her features had smeared. Pinnocchio looked down at his chest. There, on the front of his clothes, was most of the puppet's face.

"Oh, no!" he said, out loud.

"What's wrong?" called Jiminy.

"Oh, nothing," answered Pinocchio. "I just . . . um, have to fix something."

Carefully, Pinocchio repainted the puppet's face. "There," he said to himself. "She's as good as new." He set her back on the workbench and went to finish his homework.

When Geppetto returned, he found Pinocchio and Jiminy hard at work. He took off his coat and went back to his workroom.

Suddenly Geppetto called out. "Pinocchio! What were you doing while I was gone?"

"My homework, Father," answered Pinocchio.

"Is that all?" Geppetto asked.

"Of course, Father," Pinocchio replied.

He felt a funny feeling on his face, and he heard a little squeak.

Jiminy Cricket gasped. "Pinoke!" he whispered, pointing to Pinocchio's face.

"Sssh!" hissed Pinocchio.

"Are you sure that was all you did?" asked Geppetto again, coming to the door.

"Yes, Father," said Pinocchio. He felt another tweak and heard another squeak.

"Pinocchio, look at me," said Geppetto.

"Pinoke," Jiminy cried. "Your nose!"

Pinocchio looked down. Then he clapped his hands over his face.

"I don't think you are telling me the truth," said Geppetto.

"But I am," protested Pinocchio. *Pop!* His wooden nose poked through his fingers.

Pinocchio hung his head. "I tried to fix her, Father," he said.

"You have caused me extra work," said Geppetto. "You'll have to help me."

So Pinocchio worked far into the night. He scrubbed and sanded until he had cleaned the puppet's face.

"I guess you may go to bed," said Geppetto. "But I don't know what to do about your nose."

Wearily, Pinocchio dragged himself up the stairs. He knew the other children at

school would laugh at his nose. He thought
about pretending to be sick the next day,
but then he remembered. That would be
telling a lie, and lying had already got him
in trouble. With a sigh, he went to sleep.

Later that night, Pinocchio woke up.
There was a light at his window. "Jiminy,"
he called. "What's going on?"

Jiminy Cricket sat up. "I don't believe it!"
he said.

"Is it you, Blue Fairy?" said Pinocchio.
"Gosh, I'm glad to see . . ." Then he
remembered his nose. He tried to hide
under the covers.

"I see you haven't been telling the truth,"
said the fairy.

"No, ma'am," said Pinocchio.

"What have you learned?" she asked.

Pinocchio thought. Then he said, "It's
always better to tell the truth."

"Ma'am," said Jiminy Cricket, "what
about his nose?"

"Yes, I should fix that," the fairy said.
"He has learned his lesson." She waved her
magic wand.

In a flash, Pinocchio's nose went back to its normal size. "Oh, thank you, Blue Fairy!" he cried.

"You're welcome," she replied. "Now go to sleep, and remember—no more lies."

The next morning, Geppetto noticed Pinocchio's nose right away. "What has happened?" he said.

"The Blue Fairy came last night," said Pinocchio, "and she waved her wand, and she fixed my nose, and . . . "

"Yes, yes," said Geppetto, impatiently. "And she gave you a pot of gold, too. Pinocchio, why won't you tell the truth?"

"That is the truth, Father," said the little puppet.

Then Geppetto realized something—Pinocchio's nose wasn't growing.

Geppetto smiled. "I guess you have learned your lesson."

"Yes, Father," said Pinocchio. "I will never tell another lie."

Jiminy Cricket made a little squeak. Pinocchio gasped and felt his nose.

"Just joking, Pinoke," chuckled Jiminy.

Suited for Space

In February 1984, astronaut Bruce McCandless II stepped out of the shuttle *Challenger* as it orbited around the earth and floated free in space. He was wearing a pressurized space suit and a jet-propelled backpack whose 24 jet thrusters let him maneuver in space in any direction he wanted to go. This was the first time that an astronaut left the shuttle without being connected to it by a safety line. On later flights, other astronauts—including Dr. Kathryn Sullivan, the first woman to walk in space—have also used the backpack.

Space suit and backpack (below) let astronauts leave shuttle to work in space (left).

EARLY SPACE SUITS

The space suit on the left had its own solar-powered headpiece. The suit was made of metal reflecting "scales" designed to protect against the sun's rays. The suit on the right was designed to let moon explorers stop and rest. The legs extended to become a seat.

The success of the backpack, called a manned maneuvering unit (MMU), means that astronauts now have the ability to do work in space outside of their spacecraft.

The astronaut maneuvers in space by using joysticks on the arms of the backpack. The space suit's nine layers keep out the sun's harmful radiation. The "Snoopy Hat," or Communications Carrier, lets the astronaut talk to other astronauts.

On February 7, 1984, Bruce McCandless II became the first astronaut to walk in space (below).

Pied Piper of Pop

What is Michael Jackson really like?

Onstage, this superstar delights in using his enormous talent to entertain his fans. Offstage, he seems to be something of a mystery. When he's not performing, he spends most of his time hidden from public view at his estate near Los Angeles.

Friends say that there really isn't any

mystery. Very simply, Michael is a shy person who prefers to lead his own special kind of private life.

Unlike many stars, Michael doesn't smoke or drink. He's a vegetarian and a deeply religious person. But like other stars, he has filled his life with very special things. His home looks like a castle. One room is crammed with video games. Another is a

Michael (shown here with Quincy Jones) won eight Grammy awards in 1984, a record number.

movie theater with 32 seats. He can serve popcorn from his own popcorn cart or ice-cream sodas from his own soda fountain. And he keeps a whole zoo of pets, including a boa constrictor and a llama.

When he's onstage, the private Michael Jackson becomes the dazzling public performer. In 1984, Michael and four of his brothers made a "Victory Tour" to 13 U.S. cities. The tour's success was not surprising. Michael is easily the most famous pop star in the world today, so adored that his fans copy his style, wearing padded jackets and a single glove.

Now Michael seems to be ready to try new things. The Jacksons say that the Victory Tour was the last time the brothers will perform together. Michael, who appeared in the film *The Wiz*, says he'd like to appear in other movies.

Wherever he leads, his fans will surely follow.

Each of Michael's gloves has 1,200 rhinestones.

LOOSE CABOOSE

The snow started to fall when the circus ended at Corkerville. It was snowing harder as the men took down the big circus tent. Then they loaded it aboard Casey Jr., the circus train. Soon all the circus folk were on the little train. And it was still snowing.

Casey huffed and puffed out of the Corkerville station. The next stop was Middletown. Casey tooted his whistle. "It won't be an easy trip," he thought. Casey knew that soon the railroad tracks would cross the mountains. It was a tough trip in nice weather. In a snowstorm, it would be really difficult!

The little circus train started the long climb into the mountains. The snow was now a raging blizzard!

Casey puffed against the icy wind and swirling snow. His lamp was the only spot of light in the stormy night. Higher and higher he climbed. His wheels were slipping and sliding on the frozen rails.

The circus train cars behind Casey were dark. Everybody was asleep, worn out from their show in Corkerville.

In the last car of the train, Timothy and Dumbo were sleeping, too. They didn't even know there was a storm outside.

Casey Jr. was huffing and puffing to reach the top of the tallest mountain. Suddenly something terrible happened.

The coupling that held the caboose broke.
The car with Dumbo and Timothy rolled
backward. Down the steep, icy tracks it
went!

The caboose rolled faster and faster down
the mountain rails, for miles and miles.
Then, with a squishy bump, the car came to
a stop.

Timothy and Dumbo woke up.

"Hey! What's going on?" Timothy cried,
rubbing his head.

Dumbo blinked.

They both looked out the window, but
they couldn't see a thing. Timothy opened
the back door of the caboose. Snowflakes
and wind blew in.

Timothy figured out what had happened.
"I'll be darned!" he exclaimed. "We're stuck
in a snowdrift!"

Timothy closed the door to keep the snow
out. "The caboose must have come loose!"
he said. We're stranded in a blizzard!"

Dumbo didn't look worried. Surely Casey
Jr. would come back for them.

Timothy shook his head. He knew what
Dumbo was thinking. "I don't think Casey
can come back and get us," he said. "He
won't be able to back up through the snow."

Timothy closed his eyes and thought
hard. Then he looked at Dumbo. "You'll just
have to fly us out of here," he said.

Dumbo had never flown in a snowstorm
before. But what else could they do?

Timothy and Dumbo opened the caboose
door again. They went out in the whistling
wind and swirling snow.

Timothy jumped into Dumbo's hat and
held on tight. Dumbo flapped his ears. Soon
they were on their way.

But they had flown only a few feet when
Timothy felt Dumbo lurch. "Flap your ears,
Dumbo!" he cried.

But the little elephant continued to
wobble. They began to drift down.

Timothy squinted his eyes and tried to
see Dumbo's ears.

"Dumbo!" he shouted. "Your ears are
covered with ice!"

Dumbo's ears were stiff. He couldn't flap
them. Soon he and Timothy plopped down
in a snowbank.

Dumbo sat up. He shook the snow out of
his trunk.

"It's not your fault, Dumbo," Timothy said. "You tried your best! But now I'm afraid we're *really* stranded!"

"What are you two doing outside on a night like this?" said a voice out of the snowstorm.

Dumbo and Timothy looked up.

Standing on top of the snowbank, just above them, was Joe Stork.

Timothy told Joe the whole story . . . how their car came loose from the rest of the circus train . . . how they rolled down the mountain in the snowstorm . . . how Dumbo tried to fly.

"Quite a story, boys," Joe said. "But don't worry! I'll get you out of here!"

"*You?*" said Timothy. He looked from the tall, skinny bird to the short, plump elephant.

"I'll fly you out," Joe answered.

"Dumbo's a pretty good flier, but he couldn't do it," Timothy pointed out. "It's snowing too hard."

Joe thought that was pretty funny. "I deliver babies all over the world," he laughed. "I can fly in all kinds of weather." He shook his wings, showing how the snow didn't stick to him.

"Well, I know you could carry me," said Timothy. "But Dumbo's pretty heavy."

"Are you kidding? I just delivered a baby hippo to the zoo," said Joe. "Dumbo is no bigger than that."

Miles ahead on the tracks, Casey Jr. had
stopped. Everybody on the circus train
knew what had happened to Dumbo and
Timothy.

Mrs. Jumbo was terribly worried. "Can't
we go back for my baby?" she pleaded.

But the other elephants shook their heads sadly. "All we can do is wait for the storm to stop," they said.

All of a sudden, the door to the elephant car flew open. In came Joe Stork, carrying Dumbo and Timothy in a baby-bundle. He set them down on the floor.

"Dumbo! Timothy! How glad I am to see you!" Mrs. Jumbo exclaimed.

Timothy told Dumbo's mother how Joe Stork had rescued them.

"Well," said Mrs. Jumbo, "I guess this is the first time the stork has delivered the same baby *twice!*"

OLYMPIC
MOMENTS, 1984

Win or lose, the men and women who competed in the 1984 Olympic Games tested their skill and desire against outstanding athletes from all over the world. Once again, this dazzling sporting event provided spectators with memorable moments of excitement and drama, disappointment and triumph.

The Winter Games, held in snowy Sarajevo, Yugoslavia, featured a pointy-nosed wolf named Vuko as the official mascot. The Soviet Union won the most medals—25, while East Germany had the most golds—nine. The United States won eight medals, four of them gold, and Canada won four medals, two of them gold.

The Summer Games, held in Los Angeles, began under the shadow of a boycott by the Soviet Union and 13 other nations. But despite this, the Summer Olympics gathered together more athletes—7,575—from more countries—140—than any previous Olympics.

Left, the opening day ceremonies at Los Angeles.

Greg Louganis (above) won two gold medals in diving. Track star Carl Lewis (right) equaled Jesse Owens' record by winning four events.

The colorful pageantry of the opening and closing ceremonies was a fitting frame for the athletic contests. In 24 events, from gymnastics to judo, from weight lifting to

water polo, the athletes at Los Angeles put on a brilliant show of competitive excellence. The United States ended up with a record total of 83 gold medals and 174 medals in all. Canada had the fourth highest total, with 44 medals, 10 of them gold.

Mary Lou Retton, the first American to win the individual all-around gold medal in gymnastics

Animal Champions

There are no Olympics for animals, but there are animal champions. Experts don't always agree on exactly how far an animal can leap or how fast it can run, swim, or fly. But scientists have learned a great deal about the amazing abilities of animals and how they compare to those of humans.

Swimming Champions
(The fastest swimmer in the Olympics reached a top speed of about 5 miles an hour).
Sea Otter: 10 miles per hour.
Walrus: 15 miles per hour.
Sea Turtle: 22 miles per hour.
Dolphin and Whale: 25 miles per hour and higher.

Running Champ: the cheetah (above).

Long Leaper: the kangaroo.

Penguin: 30 miles per hour.
Shark: 40 miles per hour.
Swordfish: 58 miles per hour.
The Champion Swimmer—Sailfish: 60 miles per hour
(about twice the speed of a nuclear submarine).

Running Champions
(The top speed for an Olympic runner is 27 miles per hour.)
Charging Rhinoceros: 28 miles per hour.
Galloping Grizzly: 30 miles per hour.
Cat Chasing Mouse: 30 miles per hour.
Lion: 36 miles per hour.
Greyhound: 41.7 miles per hour.
Racehorse: 43.3 miles per hour.
Ostrich: 43.5 miles per hour.
The Running Champion—Cheetah: 71 miles
per hour.

Agile Animals: the penguin and the grizzly bear.

Flying Champions
Wandering Albatross: 77 miles per hour.
Golden Eagle: 80 miles per hour.
Racing Pigeon: 90 miles per hour.
Spine-tailed Swift: 106 miles per hour.
The Flying Champion—Falcon in a Power Dive:
240 miles per hour.

Jumping Champions
*(The Olympic record for the long jump is 29 feet,
2½ inches.)*
Jumping Horse: 27.25 feet.
Impala: 35 feet.
Mountain Lion: 39 feet.
The Champion Jumper—Kangaroo: 42 feet.
The Champion Jumper for Its Size—Flea: 13 inches.
This is 200 times the length of a flea's body. A
kangaroo jumps about 8 times the length of its body.

Cars of the Future.

What will the cars of the future be like? No one knows for sure. But engineers, designers, and car companies are now working on models of future cars that promise to make driving 30 years from now quite different from driving today. These future cars will use television, radar, computers, and space satellites to make a motorist's life safer and easier.

Cars of the future will be rounder and smoother in shape than today's cars. This will cut down wind resistance and save fuel. Lighter parts made of tough space-age plastics will also save fuel. And some cars of the future may burn alcohol or natural gas instead of gasoline.

Future cars will offer great advances in convenience. For example, they might have

Two versions of future cars from Ford: the Probe IV (left) and a three-wheeled commuter car (below).

Future cars may have dashboard TV (left). GM's Lean Machine tilts going around curves (right).

an engine that pops out for easy servicing. A driver could drop the engine off at the service station and plug in a spare engine.

Computers will constantly monitor the car's performance. If something is wrong, the computer will tell the driver—probably using a human voice! In fact, the computer will tell the driver everything he or she needs to know, from information about speed and fuel to weather conditions ahead.

The car's computer may also communicate with a satellite that would radio back the car's position. This would be shown on a dashboard video map, so the driver would know the car's exact location.

Cars of the future may also use radar or other sensing devices to keep track of cars or other objects on the highway ahead. The sensing devices will receive information electronically from cables buried in the roads. The sensors will use the information to steer the car down the highway automatically, while the driver sips coffee and reads the morning paper.

Aero 2000, on view at EPCOT Center, is an experimental future car developed by GM.

A Cow of a Different Color

"Easy, Belle," said Huey, patting the cow's shoulder as he brushed her neck.

"Yeah, Belle," said Dewey. "You want to look nice for the fair tomorrow, don't you?"

"Sure, she does," put in Louie. "She's going to win a ribbon."

"Now, boys," said Grandma Duck. "Don't count your ribbons before you win them."

The three Junior Woodchucks had spent

the summer at Grandma's farm. They brushed Belle and exercised her. They fed her the very best hay and grain. If ever a cow was healthy and clean, it was Belle.

Now they filled Belle's stall with sweet-smelling straw and put hay in her manger. Then they gave her a good-night pat.

As they walked toward the house, they didn't see the shadowy figure creeping in the barn door.

The next morning, Huey, Dewey, and
Louie jumped out of bed and scrambled into
their clothes. Out to the barn they ran.

In the barn, they skidded to a stop. There
was Belle's stall, but Belle wasn't in it!

"Did we leave the door open?" asked
Huey. His brothers shook their heads.

"We've got to find her," said Louie.

But Belle was nowhere to be found.

"I'm sorry, boys," said Grandma. "We
don't have any more time to look for her.
The fair starts in an hour, and I have to
take my entries in. Are you coming?"

"Sure, Grandma," sighed Huey. "We'll
help you carry your jellies and pickles."

So they all piled into Grandma Duck's old
car and headed for the Duckburg County
Fair.

Grandma's apricot and raspberry jellies took first and second prize. And the pickle judge gave the blue ribbon to her sweet pickle relish.

"Gosh, Grandma," said Dewey. "Two ribbons! That's great!"

"Thank you, boys," replied Grandma. "Now, why don't you see something of the fair? They have a Tilt-A-Whirl and a Dragon Maze."

"Maybe later, Grandma," said Louie. "Some of the other Junior Woodchucks are

showing their cows, and we want to wish
them luck."

"That's a fine idea," said Grandma. "I'll
meet you at the dairy barn later."

As Huey, Dewey, and Louie walked
through the dairy barn, other children were
brushing their cows' coats and fluffing their
cows' tails. The boys felt sad—they should
have been brushing and fluffing, too.

Suddenly they heard a lot of noise. A cow
was kicking and shaking her head. Finally
the rope that tied her snapped.

The cow came running at Huey, Dewey, and Louie. They stretched out their arms to keep her from stampeding out of the barn. But when the cow got to Huey, she stopped. "Moo!" she cried, and she gave him a big lick on the cheek.

"What on earth?!" said Dewey. The cow looked at him and gave him a lick too.

"This cow acts like Belle," said Louie, as

the strange cow rubbed up against his arm.
"But her spots are all wrong."

Then Huey looked at Louie's sleeve,
where the cow had touched him. "Maybe
those aren't her real spots," he said. "Come
on."

They were met by a sour-faced fellow
named Lonnie. "What are you doing with
my cow?" he demanded.

"I think we should ask you the same
thing," said Huey. He picked up a red rag
and dipped it in a bucket of water.

"What do you mean?" said Lonnie.

Huey rubbed at a patch of white on the
cow's coat. As he rubbed, the white spot
became gray, and the red rag became pink.
"This is our cow," he said.

"She is not," blustered Lonnie.

"Prove it!" challenged Louie.

"How?" said Lonnie.

"Give her a bath," said Dewey.

Lonnie was caught. If he washed the cow,
her extra spots would come off.

"You win," he said. "She is your cow. I
painted extra spots on her with white shoe
polish, so you wouldn't know her."

"But why did you do it?" asked Huey.

"I had no chance against the Woodchucks
with my own cow," Lonnie said.

Just then, Grandma walked up. "What's going on, boys?" she asked.

When they had explained what had happened, they were surprised. They thought Grandma would be mad. Instead, she looked sad.

"How long have you lived in Duckburg, Lonnie?" she asked.

Lonnie hung his head. "Since May."

Grandma turned to the boys. "Did you ever invite Lonnie to join the Junior Woodchucks?" she asked.

"Well, no," said Dewey. "But . . . "

"But you should have," Grandma said. "If you had been more friendly, this would never have happened."

It was the boys' turn to hang their heads.

Then Louie held out his hand to Lonnie. "Sorry," he said. "I bet it wasn't much fun being left out."

"I'm sorry, too," said Lonnie, shaking Louie's hand.

"Well, now," said Grandma, "why don't you all give Belle a good bath. The judging is in an hour."

Lonnie picked up a bucket. "I'll help," he offered, "if you don't mind."

"We need all the help we can get," said Huey.

Grandma watched the boys take Belle off to wash her.

"Listen, Lonnie," Huey was saying, "after the judging is over, why don't you come with us on the Super Slide?"

"Yeah," said Dewey, "and then we can all get some Pepper Bellies to eat."

"And some Krispy Kritters for dessert," Louie added. "Grandma," he called back to her, "can we bring you some Pepper Bellies and Krispy Kritters?"

Grandma Duck laughed. "No, thanks," she answered. "I think I'll just have a cup of tea and some oatmeal cookies."

CLICK!
It's a Photograph

Togetherness, *by Jeff Kozlowski, 17, Wausau, Wisconsin.*

Grandma's corner, *by Terri Piekut, 17, Cicero, New York.*

Untitled, *by Kerry Green, 17, Lakewood, Colorado.*

The photographer looks through the camera's viewfinder and sees a "picture"— of two boys in sunglasses, an ancient watering can, some zebra-striped glasses. The photographer clicks the shutter, and the picture becomes a photograph to remember.

Blinded, *by Tyler Smith, 17, Naples, Florida.*

Untitled, *by Sean Oertle, 17, Provo, Utah.*

The photographs on these pages were among the winners in the 1984 Scholastic/Kodak Photo Award Program. This program is open to students in junior and senior high schools in the United States and Canada. The winners receive scholarships and other awards.

Make a Mark

Bookmarks are useful. They mark your place in a book you haven't finished. They're also fun to make and to give as presents.

STARS AND STRIPES

What You'll Need

Ribbons of different widths, stickers, construction paper, glue, scissors.

What To Do

1. Cut equal lengths of three ribbons. Glue the pieces together, with the narrowest ribbon on top.
2. Glue stars or stickers or construction paper designs on the front and back.

RAINBOW RIBBONS

These bookmarks can be used to mark several pages in a book at the same time.

What You'll Need

Paper, felt, ribbons, glue, scissors.

What To Do

1. Draw an animal or other design on a piece of paper. Cut out the paper design and use it as a pattern to make two felt pieces. Draw in details such as eyes and a mouth with a felt-tipped pen.
2. Cut three ribbons of different lengths. Put the shorter lengths on top.
3. Glue one piece of the felt design onto the front of the ribbons and the other piece onto the back.

PAPER CLIPS

These bookmarks work like a paper clip, with the "tongue" on one side of the page and the rest of the bookmark on the other side.

What You'll Need

Construction paper, scissors, crayons or felt-tipped pens.

What To Do

1. Draw the shape of the bookmark on the construction paper and cut it out.

2. Cut out a tongue like the tongues shown. Decorate with crayons or pen.

Butterflies and Sandy Eyes

Do you ever blush bright pink or get
"goose bumps"? And do you ever wonder
why this happens? The answer is that your
body reacts physically to your experiences—
your body "talks back" to you.

Blushing
When someone says or does something
that makes you feel uncomfortable or

embarrassed, your face may turn bright pink.

When you are embarrassed, you get excited. Your brain tells your heart to pump faster, and your heart sends extra blood to your body. The blood that rushes to your face makes your skin turn pink.

Mouth Watering

When you smell cookies or a hamburger, you may notice that your mouth is "watering"—it has filled with saliva.

This happens because your brain remembers that cookies are a favorite food. Your brain prepares your body for eating the cookies by telling glands near your mouth to begin producing saliva. Saliva moistens food and makes it easier to swallow. It also contains chemicals that help you digest food.

Goose Bumps

Most of your body is covered with tiny hairs. Each hair has a tiny muscle at its

base. If you get cold, this muscle tightens up. This stops the loss of heat from your body. It also makes the hair stand up, forming the bumps called "goose bumps." You can also get goose bumps when you're nervous. Your body then produces adrenaline, a chemical which tightens the hair muscles.

Butterflies in Your Stomach

Your stomach moves constantly, churning food and pushing it down the stomach.   If you get upset, your brain may tell your stomach muscles to stop working. This saves energy. The other muscles in your body then have enough energy to deal with what has upset you. When your stomach suddenly stops, you feel as if butterflies were flying around inside you.

Sand in Your Eyes

Tears are a liquid that contains salt and other chemicals. This liquid is produced by glands behind the eyelids.

When you are asleep, the liquid collects in the corners of your eyes. As you sleep, the liquid gradually dries out.

The chemicals are left behind, and they form crusty, sticky grains of "sand."

ZZZZZZZZZZZZZZ
(Animal Style)

Just like you, most kinds of animals need periods of sleep each day. But you'll find some of their sleeping habits—and their bedrooms—surprising. A tree frog, for example, will fall asleep in the middle of the day, right in the branches of a tree. Like most amphibians, the tree frog sleeps very lightly and does not dream. The slightest noise will wake it. Birds and mammals, like

The koala (left) and the dormouse (right) are caught napping—a favorite pastime.

people, sleep more deeply. Mammals dream, and scientists think that birds may have very short dreams, too.

Some animals can sleep almost anywhere. Sea lions stretch out and doze off on a bed of hard rocks. The sea otter likes to float lazily on its back and be lulled to sleep by the waves.

Most birds are active during the day and doze in the trees at night. But some birds,

The saw-whet owl takes his daily doze.

The sea otter grabs forty winks in the water.

such as owls, sleep during the day and hunt
for food at night. Many birds fall asleep
while firmly grasping a tree branch, often
with one leg.

Some animals sleep for months at a time.
These animals hibernate during the cold
winter months. Hibernation is different
from true sleep. The animal's body
temperature drops and its heartbeat and

breathing slow down much more than they do in sleep. This means that the animal uses much less energy. It can live for months on fat stored in its body.

The dormouse is a famous hibernator. The dormouse prepares for winter by eating as much as it can and getting fat. Then it curls up in a snug den and snoozes the winter away. When it wakes up in the spring, it may have lost half of its weight.

Some animals can sleep almost anywhere: tree frogs choose trees, sea lions snooze on rocks.

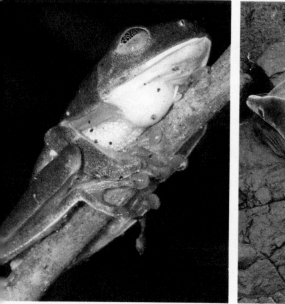

Jon and the Three Wishes

Once upon a time there was a young man
named Jon. He worked very hard on his
farm. But he was still very poor.

One evening he was coming home from
his field, and he saw a strange glow. He
went to look at it.

It came from the middle of some bushes. Peeking over them, Jon saw a wonderful sight. There were many tiny people, dressed in green and red. They were having a feast.

Some of the little people began to play a lively tune. All the others danced happily in the moonlight.

Jon tapped his foot in time to the music. Before he knew it, he was clapping his hands. When the little people heard him, everything vanished—tables, food, dancers, and musicians.

"It was a fairy feast," Jon thought.

Suddenly he saw a light in one of the bushes. He bent down to see better and found a fairy caught in the brambles by her long golden hair.

The more she pulled and tugged, the more she became entangled.

"Poor thing," thought Jon. He pulled out his knife and cut her free.

"Oh, thank you," the beautiful fairy said. "You have done me a great favor. As your reward, I will give you three wishes." She

then handed three of her golden hairs to Jon. "Hold one up at night when the moon is bright and make a wish. I will grant it." Then the fairy vanished.

When Jon got home, he hid the golden hairs under his mattress. The next day he barely remembered his adventure. Soon he forgot it altogether, which is what usually happens when people meet fairies.

Now the kind and beautiful Princess Cassie, daughter of the king, wanted to find a husband. The man would have to pass three tests, one for strength, one for courage, and one for honesty.

Knights from far and wide came to try the test of strength. But no one was able to chop down the giant tree that grew outside the castle wall.

Jon watched as one knight after another failed the test. "If only I could win," he thought. "But I'm only a humble farmer. I don't have the strength of a knight."

Then one day Jon was working in the field. He saw the princess out walking. She was very beautiful. Jon stared at her long golden hair.

Then he remembered. "The fairy queen's three wishes!" he said to himself. "They can help me."

That night when the moon was out, Jon held up one of the golden strands. "Help me cut down the giant tree and marry the princess," he said.

There was a flash, and then a magic axe lay in Jon's hand.

The next morning he went to the tree. He swung the enchanted axe with all his strength.

There was a great crack and groan. Then came a crash that shook the ground for miles around. The tree had fallen.

Jon was summoned before the king, who praised his strength. But Jon wasn't listening. His eyes were on the fair Cassie. She was looking at Jon. It was plain to see that they were falling in love.

"For the test of courage," announced the king, "you will spend the night in the haunted wood. If you are still there in the morning, you will have proved you are brave."

When she heard this, the princess fainted. She knew that no one had ever spent the night in the haunted wood and lived.

That evening as the moon rose high, Jon held up the second of the fairy's golden hairs. "Help me spend the night in the haunted wood so I can win the hand of the princess."

Again there was a flash, and Jon was holding a fairy charm. It was three twigs tied together with a red ribbon. Jon tucked it in his pocket and went to the haunted wood.

The wood was a dark, foul-smelling place.
But Jon didn't feel frightened. He had the
fairy charm, after all. So he curled up under
a tree and fell fast asleep.

When Jon awoke the next morning, he heard the birds chirping and saw sunlight shining through the trees. The haunted wood was now a beautiful wood.

Jon sat down to wait for the king.

When the king found Jon, he was surprised. He thought that Jon couldn't live through a night in the haunted wood.

"You've done far better than I expected," said the king. "Come to the castle tomorrow for the test of honesty."

That night John held up the last golden hair. "Help me win the test of honesty so I can marry the princess," he said.

This time the fairy queen appeared to Jon and handed him a small cake. "Whoever eats this can only see and say the truth," she said. Then she vanished.

The next morning Jon stood before the princess and the king with the small cake in his hand.

"Now for the test of honesty," said the king. "Answer me this: did you pass the tests of strength and courage all on your own?"

Jon was naturally a truthful person. He didn't need the help of the magic cake to tell the king about the fairy, the axe, and the charm, so he replied, "No, I didn't."

"Ha!" cried the king with a sly smile. "That disqualifies you!"

The princess began to cry. But suddenly the king saw the fairy cake in Jon's hand. He couldn't help himself. He grabbed the cake and ate it.

Then the king, too, began to weep. "I was afraid my daughter would marry and leave me all alone," he cried. "So I made up a contest that no one would win. But now I know how selfish I have been.

"You are a strong, courageous, and truthful man. Most important of all, my daughter loves you and you love her. I will be very happy if you marry."

Not long after that, Jon and Princess Cassie were married. And since Jon had no kingdom of his own, he came to live at the castle, and the king was never lonely. And they all lived happily ever after.